Love Peace Wealth Prosperity

Vaccinate The Mind
in 44 Days

Illustrated & Designed by: Tanisha White

Acknowledgements: Dr. James Beard, Les Brown, Inky Johnson, Eric Thomas, Earl Nightingale, and Napoleon Hill.

Volume 1

For Your Thoughts

LOVE • PEACE • WEALTH • PROSPERITY

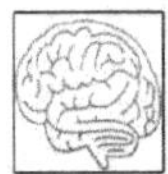

"I believe in you. Most people will spend
their entire lives reflecting on things they
could of done differently, so do things right
today instead of tomorrow. If you can see
the moon you can see the future. Always
invest in you for a greater opportunity."

Sunday 4:21 p.m.

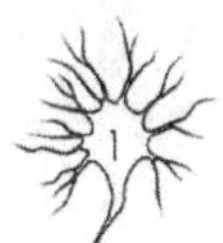

LOVE • PEACE • WEALTH • PROSPERITY

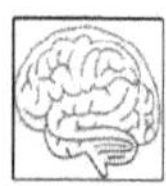

"Trust the process don't rush the process."

Monday 6:15 a.m.

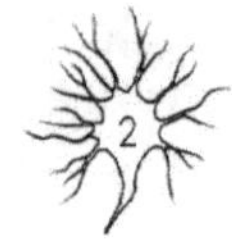

LOVE • PEACE • WEALTH • PROSPERITY

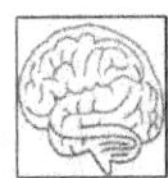

"The best things in life are not things."

Tuesday 7:01 a.m.

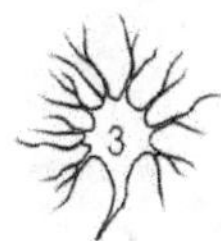

LOVE · PEACE · WEALTH · PROSPERITY

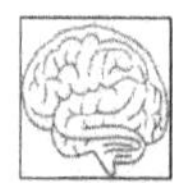

"Self sabotage is your biggest hater."

Wednesday 1:45 p.m.

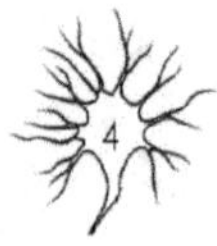

LOVE • PEACE • WEALTH • PROSPERITY

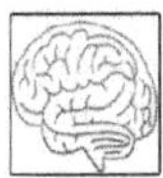

"When you start being happy for others,
you'll start being happy."

Thursday 12:58 p.m.

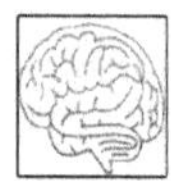

"Create opportunities don't wait for them.
Take the first step with less timorousness and
commence your journey. Faith is dead
without action."

Friday 9:01 p.m.

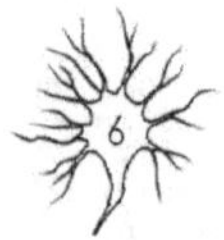

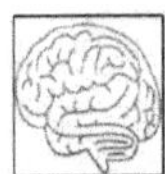

Look in the mirror and face who you really
are. Recite out loud;
"I AM STRONG, SMART, AND POWERFUL!"

Saturday 5:32 a.m.

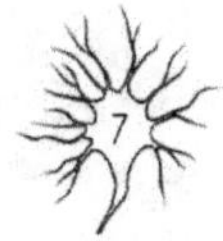

LOVE • PEACE • WEALTH • PROSPERITY

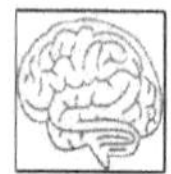

"Just because you can't see the air,
doesn't stop you from breathing. Always
believe in yourself."

Saturday 3:58 p.m.

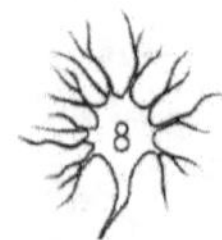

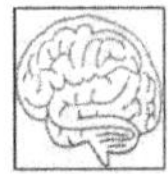

"I once was a product of my environment, surrounded by a different energy. Now I'm in the league of millionaires. Surround yourself with like minded people."

Sunday 6:20 p.m.

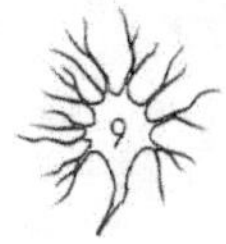

LOVE ▪ PEACE ▪ WEALTH ▪ PROSPERITY

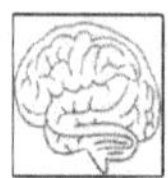

"The decisions you make today will support
you tomorrow negative or positive. Learn
how to pick your battles in life because
some mistakes may shadow you forever. Be
conscious of your decisions and how they
may affect others. "

Monday 6:11 a.m.

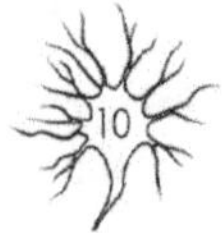

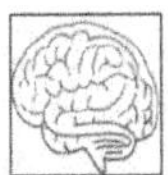

" If you're too busy focusing on the things
you don't value, you'll forget about the
things you do value. "

Time
Space
Energy
Matter
Thought

Tuesday 3:57 p.m.

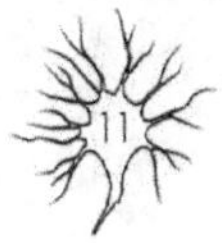

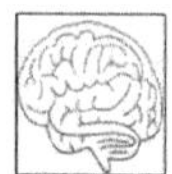

Practice positive affirmations; "I am proud
of myself for the things I've accomplished
thus far." Personal growth and the
development of more brain cells will
enhance your vision and goals.

Friday 8:40 a.m.

For Your Thoughts

LOVE • PEACE • WEALTH • PROSPERITY

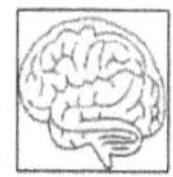

"I am a BOSS, I don't have restrictions."

Saturday 8:32 p.m.

LOVE • PEACE • WEALTH • PROSPERITY

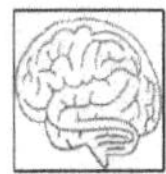

When you hold yourself back with fear, you
will be left with unanswered questions.
"What if you've lived your whole life just to
feel incomplete, and that it was all a lie?"

Sunday 7:43 a.m.

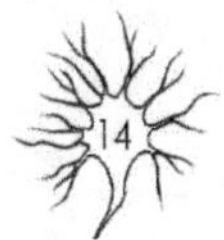

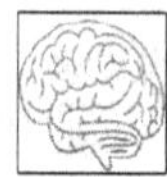

"Success comes to those who become successful conscious. On the contrary, failure comes to those who indifferently allow themselves to become failure-conscious. Act as if it's completely impossible to fail."

Monday 11:35 a.m.

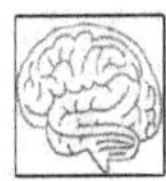

"No more excuses and no more bullshit."

Tuesday 10:59 p.m.

LOVE • PEACE • WEALTH • PROSPERITY

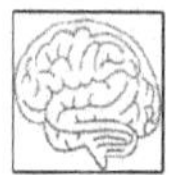

"If you think about nothing you become
nothing. The things we get for nothing
we can't get back."

Wednesday 7:28 a.m.

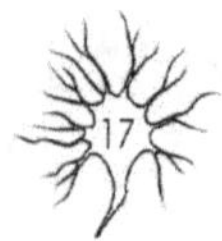

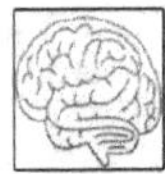

"The last time I lied I died a little."

Thursday 8:41 a.m.

LOVE • PEACE • WEALTH • PROSPERITY

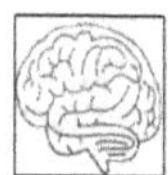

"Success isn't something you were born
with; it's something that you have to create.
Stop thinking about all the reasons why
you're not successful."

Friday 11:16 p.m.

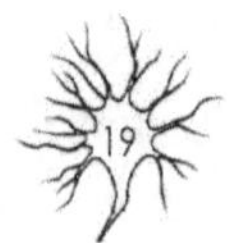

LOVE • PEACE • WEALTH • PROSPERITY

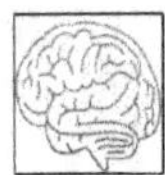

"We all have the same 24 hours, but it's completely up to you how you value and utilize that Eighty Six Thousand and Four Hundred seconds each day."

Saturday 3:09 a.m.

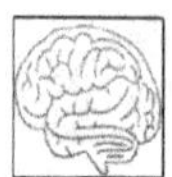

"Don't let the past affect your
present. Reach for the moon and stay on
course. Be brave and take risks.
A winner is someone that
is brave enough to try one more time."

Sunday 4:44 p.m.

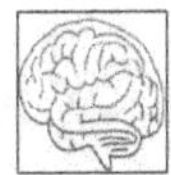

"Hack your mind for knowledge; you can't be arrested for something that's yours to plunder."

Monday 7:17 a.m.

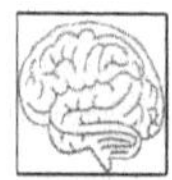

"Being healthy is not a sprint it's a marathon.
Health is wealth."

Tuesday 10:51 a.m.

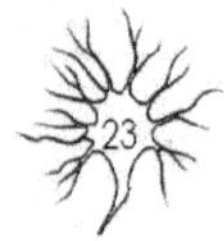

LOVE • PEACE • WEALTH • PROSPERITY

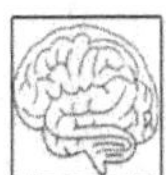

"You can't always control the downs,
but you sure can control the ups
with hard work."

Wednesday 1:11 p.m.

LOVE • PEACE • WEALTH • PROSPERITY

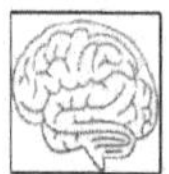

"You must give everyone the best
version of you."

Thursday 8:19 a.m.

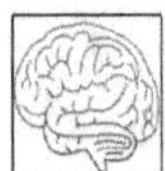

"Love the process. You're never suppose to wish for it more then when you work for it. The harder you work the harder it'll be to surrender."

Friday 6:45 p.m.

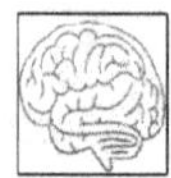

"Prepare yourself for the things you
dreamed for."

Saturday 8:02 a.m.

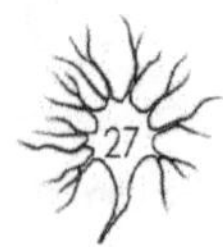

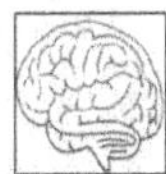

"Stop being selfish and learn how to become a team player because anyone can be replaced. There is no "I" in Team."

Sunday 6:56 p.m.

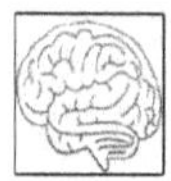

"Head up, chest out, and walk with
a purpose. "

Monday 7:53 a.m.

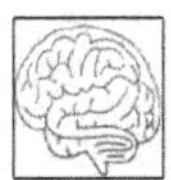

"When you find yourself drowning without a
life jacket, there's always someone to save
you if you just open your eyes."

Tuesday 12:33 p.m.

For Your Thoughts

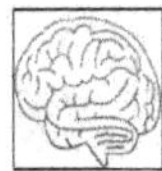

"Your only limitations are those that you
create in your own mind."

Friday 1:56 p.m.

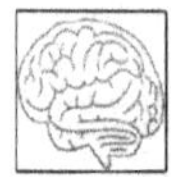

"The legacy you leave is irreplaceable.
When I die I will still be alive"

Saturday 2:22 p.m.

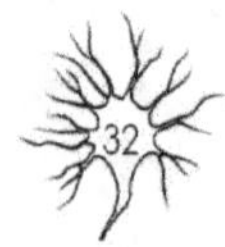

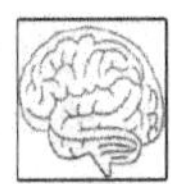

"Think big and dream bigger."

Sunday 3:34 a.m.

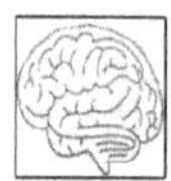

"Walk confidently and exude the type of positive energy you want reciprocated."

Monday 1:19 p.m.

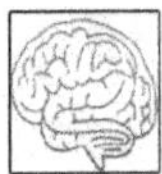

"Even the most powerful human beings on
the planet have feelings that need
validation."

Tuesday 4:54 p.m.

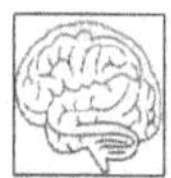

"No friends are better than fake friends that bring you down."

Wednesday 7:07 a.m.

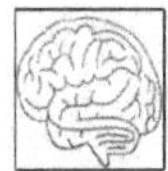

"Forgiving yourself and forgiving others will
set you up for personal growth.
Forgiveness is not for others, it's for you
to heal those wounds that have
been buried deep over time."

Thursday 6:56 a.m.

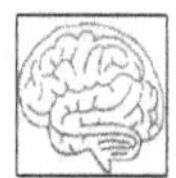

"To whom this may concern,
I can't breathe, I can't breathe,
I can't breathe!
Cherish your life you only have one."

Friday 3:00 p.m.

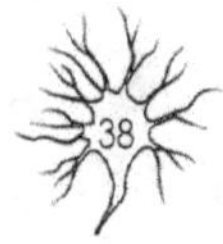

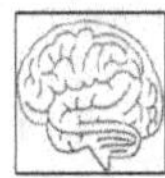

"I woke up this morning pondering the question, how can I make someone else's day better?"

Saturday 7:29 a.m.

LOVE • PEACE • WEALTH • PROSPERITY

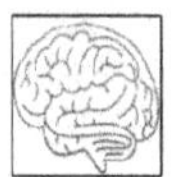

"There's only one of you and millions of
them, I dare you to be different."

Sunday 5:55 p.m.

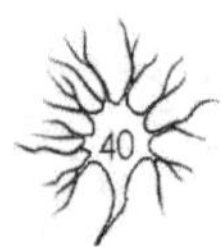

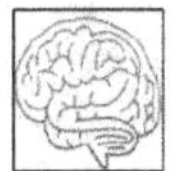

Good morning, it's a new day. Let's not let
past burdens and missteps dictate
future progress. Focus on creating new
opportunities by, feeling alive, feeling
blessed, feeling free, feeling beautiful,
and feeling worthy."I believe in you!"

Monday 7:27 a.m.

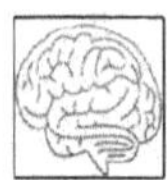

"There's no set date to resolute a problem.
Be steadfast and forthright for as long as
needed to reach the positive
outcome you seek."

Tuesday 8:50 p.m.

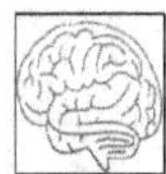

You can place a single dirty glass around four clean glasses and watch that dirty glass become clean. "Keep your circle clean."

Wednesday 2:22 p.m.

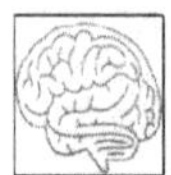

"Learn how to refill your significant others LOVE tank with the right measurements. This careful attention to detail will only ensure both parties feel complete."

Thursday 9:30 p.m.

LOVE • PEACE • WEALTH • PROSPERITY

For Your Thoughts